STARS OF MAJOR LEAGUE BASEBALL

By Craig Calcaterra

Abbeville kids
An Imprint of Abbeville Press
New York · London

Statistics are current as of October 5, 2022.
Please note: This book has not been authorized by Major League Baseball.

Project editor: Lauren Orthey
Copy editor: Ashley Benning
Layout: Ada Rodriguez
Production director: Louise Kurtz

PHOTOGRAPHY CREDITS

Adobe Stock: front cover background (© LeArchitecto); pp. 2–3 (© ronniechua); pp. 4–5 (© Michael Flippo); pp. 62–63 (© Don Mroczkowski)

Flickr: p. 49 and back cover (All-Pro Reels)

Icon Sportswire: front cover left (Cliff Welch); p. 7 (Cliff Welch); p. 9 (Joe Robbins); p. 11 (Peter Joneleit); p. 13 (Joe Robbins); p. 15 (Leslie Plaza Johnson); p. 17 and back cover (Melissa Tamez); p. 19 (David J. Griffin); p. 21 and back cover (Brian Rothmuller); p. 23 (Mark Goldman); p. 25 (David J. Griffin); pp. 27, 29 (Brian Rothmuller); p. 31 (Cliff Welch); p. 33 (Gerry Angus); p. 35 and front cover right (Brandon Sloter); p. 39 (Joe Robbins); p. 41 and front cover middle (John Cordes); p. 43 (Cliff Welch); p. 45 (Joe Robbins); p. 47 (Brian Rothmuller); p. 51 (Leslie Plaza Johnson); p. 53 (Brian Rothmuller); pp. 55, 57 (Joe Robbins); p. 59 (Brian Rothmuller); p. 61 (Frank Jansky)

Wikimedia Commons: p. 37 (Keith Allison/CC-SA-2.0)

First edition

10 9 8 7 6 5 4 3 2 1

Library of Congress Cataloging-in-Publication Data

Names: Calcaterra, Craig (Sportswriter) author.
Title: Stars of Major League Baseball / by Craig Calcaterra.
Description: First edition. | New York, N.Y. : Abbeville Press Publishers, [2023] | Audience: Ages 9–12 | Audience: Grades 4–6 | Summary: "Profiles of 28 of the greatest players in Major League Baseball"– Provided by publisher.
Identifiers: LCCN 2022053311 | ISBN 9780789214591 (hardback)
Subjects: LCSH: Baseball players–United States–Biography–Juvenile literature.
Classification: LCC GV865.A1 C315 2023 | DDC 796.3570922 [B]–dc23/eng/20221107
LC record available at https://lccn.loc.gov/2022053311

For bulk and premium sales and for text adoption procedures, write to Customer Service Manager, Abbeville Press, 655 Third Avenue, New York, NY 10017, or call 1-800-Artbook.

Visit Abbeville Kids online at www.abbevillefamily.com.

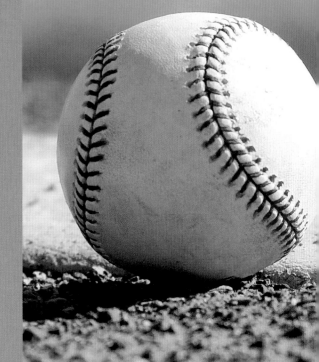

CONTENTS

José Abreu	6	Aaron Judge	36
Ronald Acuña Jr.	8	Manny Machado	38
Sandy Alcántara	10	Shohei Ohtani	40
Pete Alonso	12	José Ramírez	42
Yordan Álvarez	14	Austin Riley	44
Tim Anderson	16	Julio Rodríguez	46
Nolan Arenado	18	Max Scherzer	48
Mookie Betts	20	Corey Seager	50
Gerrit Cole	22	Juan Soto	52
Jacob deGrom	24	Fernando Tatís Jr.	54
Edwin Díaz	26	Mike Trout	56
Freddie Freeman	28	Trea Turner	58
Paul Goldschmidt	30	Justin Verlander	60
Vladimir Guerrero Jr.	32		
Bryce Harper	34	Statistics Glossary	62

José Abreu

José Abreu was already a star before anyone in the United States had even heard of him. He achieved stardom in his native Cuba where he played nearly 10 seasons, setting the Cuban home run record in 2010–11 en route to being named the Cuban Serie Nacional MVP in spite of missing almost a third of the season due to an injury. It can be hard for U.S.-based talent evaluators to judge Cuban talent given the relative lack of information and in-person scouting, but Abreu's exploits were so impressive that they spoke for themselves. Word of mouth only added to the picture. Those who saw Abreu play in Cuba spoke of a hitter with a consistent swing, power to all fields, patience at the plate, and an unsurpassed work ethic.

The only question was whether, like many other players around his age, he'd seek greater fame and riches in the U.S. major leagues. The baseball world got its answer when, in August 2013, Abreu, his fiancée, his parents, his sister, and her husband boarded a 20-foot boat in the dark of night and left the east coast of Cuba. Following a harrowing 12 hours at sea, Abreu and his family landed in Haiti and eventually made their way to the U.S.

After signing a $68 million deal with the Chicago White Sox before the 2014 season, Abreu became an instant superstar, hitting 36 home runs, batting .317, and posting a major league–leading .581 slugging percentage, all contributing to his becoming the runaway winner of that year's American League Rookie of the Year Award. He'd go on to drive in 100 or more runs in his first four seasons and five of his first six, leading the league in that category with 123 in 2019 and with 60 in the pandemic-shortened 2020 season. He'd win the American League MVP Award in 2020, leading the league in slugging percentage, total bases, and games played as well. In that year's postseason, he had a double and a homer among his four hits in three games as the White Sox lost a tightly fought series to the Oakland Athletics.

Now 36 years old, Abreu can be expected to begin to decline as a player, but if his 2021 and 2022 seasons are any guide, it'll be a slow tailing off as far as those things go, and he'll continue to be a force in the middle of the White Sox lineup for at least a few more years.

POSITION: FIRST BASE
BATS: RIGHT
THROWS: RIGHT
HT/WT: 6'3", 235 LB.
DEBUT: 3-31-14
TEAM: CHICAGO WHITE SOX
BORN: 1-29-87, CRUCES, CIENFUEGOS PROVINCE, CUBA

AVG	OBP	SLG	OPS+	HR	RBI
.292	.354	.506	134	243	863

Ronald Acuña Jr.

There was no player in all of Major League Baseball more heavily hyped in the spring of 2018 than Ronald Acuña Jr. Though he was only 20 years old at the time, Acuña had been a prospect since he was 15. His performance across three minor league levels in 2017—when he was just 19—earned him 2017 *Baseball America's* Minor League Player of the Year Award. With those plaudits and a skill set combining speed, power, on-base ability, and excellent outfield range, most believed it was only a matter of time before Acuña made a big impact at the big league level.

And make an impact he did. Though he was not called up by Atlanta until late April, Acuña was able to hit 26 home runs and achieve stats of .293/.366/.552 as baseball's youngest player in 2018. That earned him the Rookie of the Year Award—as well as the ire of division rival Miami Marlins. He hit seven home runs against them that year, causing frustrated Marlins pitchers to tag Acuña for some time afterward. Such a thing is not particularly friendly, of course, but it's a sure sign that a team has no other way of cooling off an opposing player.

Acuña has set all manner of records for being the youngest at various feats. In 2017 he was the youngest winner of the Arizona Fall League MVP Award. In 2018 he became the youngest major leaguer ever to hit home runs in five consecutive games, and, that October, Acuña became the youngest player in MLB history to hit a postseason grand slam when he did so in the National League Division Series against the Los Angeles Dodgers. The following April Acuña became the youngest player to ever sign a $100 million contract extension when he and the Braves agreed to an eight-year deal. During the 2019 season he hit 41 home runs and stole 37 bases, becoming the youngest member of the exulted "30-30" club.

Acuña is no longer the youngest star in the game, but he continues to be a force for the Braves. In 2020, he batted .250/.406/.581 with 14 home runs and 29 RBIs in only 160 plate appearances, winning the Silver Slugger Award and leading the Braves to within one game of the World Series. An injury cut his 2021 season in half, yet he still hit 24 homers and was on his way to his best offensive season before he got hurt. While that forced him to watch the Braves hoist the World Series trophy from the bench that fall, Acuña is back now—he's still only 25 years old, and there will no doubt be many accomplishments and a whole lot of winning in his and the Atlanta Braves' future.

POSITION: OUTFIELD
BATS: RIGHT
THROWS: RIGHT
HT/WT: 6'0", 205 LB.
DEBUT: 4-25-18
TEAM: ATLANTA BRAVES
BORN: 12-18-97, LA GUAIRA, LA GUAIRA STATE, VENEZUELA

AVG	OBP	SLG	OPS+	HR	RBI
.277	.370	.517	133	120	296

Sandy Alcántara

Over the past 10 years or so the role of the starting pitcher has changed dramatically. Thanks to teams using relief pitchers earlier and earlier in games, starters pitch fewer innings than they used to, and someone who pitches for a complete game has become a true rarity. The days of the workhorse starting pitcher are over, but Sandy Alcántara reigns as a true throwback to the time when starters went deep into games and, sometimes, even all the way.

Originally a St. Louis Cardinals prospect, Alcántara was traded in December 2017 to the Marlins. The Cardinals had given him a taste of big league action as a reliever by then, but because of the relative lack of pitching talent in the Marlins system, Alcántara had a better shot of making it as a starter. He made his first six major league starts in 2018 and, by 2019, was a fixture in the Miami rotation. The 2019 season was a rough experience for Alcántara on occasion—he led the league in losses due in large part to poor run support by the Marlins lineup—but he did manage to pitch two complete game shutouts that season. There were 25 *teams* that did not have as many complete game shutouts from their entire pitching staff that year.

Alcántara, along with many of his teammates, started the pandemic-shortened 2020 season on the injured list battling COVID-19. As a result he made only seven starts that year. He pitched well when he was able to take the mound, however,

going 3–2, with a 3.00 ERA as the Fish managed to make the expanded playoffs. In 2021 Alcántara was back to full strength, which was reflected by his leading the league with 33 games started and tossing over 200 innings, which has become a relative rarity in Major League Baseball. In 2022 he broke out as a true ace, making it to his second All-Star Game, and once again led the league in games started, innings pitched, and batters faced en route to an amazing six complete games, including a shutout. Again, no other team in all of baseball recorded as many complete games from their entire pitching staff as Alcántara recorded on his own.

A baseball game is nine innings long. If you had to pick one pitcher in the league today to go all nine, Sandy Alcántara would be your only logical choice.

POSITION: STARTING PITCHER
BATS: RIGHT
THROWS: RIGHT
HT/WT: 6'5", 200 LB.
DEBUT: 9-3-17
TEAMS: ST. LOUIS CARDINALS (2017), MIAMI MARLINS (2018–)
BORN: 9-7-95, AZUA, AZUA PROVINCE, DOMINICAN REPUBLIC

W	L	ERA	ERA+	IP	K	BB
34	43	3.10	135	716	638	225

Pete Alonso

Power is often the last skill a hitter develops. There was no delay in that department for Pete Alonso, however, who has been a top power prospect since he was a teenager and has launched baseballs like nobody's business since his major league debut in 2019.

Alonso was a second-round draft pick out of the University of Florida and wasted no time making an impact in professional baseball, batting .321 with 5 homers and 21 RBI in just 30 games for the Brooklyn Cyclones of the New York-Penn League. He began the 2017 season with the St. Lucie Mets of the Florida State League, continued to dominate opposing pitching, and earned a late season promotion to the Binghamton Rumble Ponies of the Eastern League, compiling a combined line of .289/.359/.524 with 27 doubles and 18 homers in 93 games. He began the 2018 season at a blistering pace, earning yet another promotion, this time to the Las Vegas 51s of the Pacific Coast League. That season he was named to the United States team for the 2018 Futures Game, during which he hit a long home run which sealed a 10–6 win for the U.S. squad. In 132 games between Binghamton and Las Vegas that year he hit .285/.395/.571 with 36 homers and 119 RBI.

With his minor league accomplishments, it was clear that Alonso was ready for the big leagues, but the big leagues were in no way ready for what he had in store for them during his rookie campaign in 2019. That year Alonso set the record for most home runs by a rookie with 53 and set franchise records for extra-base hits (85), total bases (348), and hits (155) by a rookie in a single season while batting .260/.358/.941. He was an easy choice for National League Rookie of the Year and earned a trip to the All-Star Game.

Since then, Alonso has established himself as the offensive centerpiece of the New York Mets and one of the most fearsome power hitters in the game. In his four full seasons in the big leagues he has hit 146 home runs and has driven in 380. In 2022 he led the Mets to their first post-season appearance since 2016 while setting the team's season record for RBI. And, of course, he was named an All-Star once again.

The scary part: as the 2023 season begins Alonso is still only 28 years old, giving him years and years to continue rewriting the record books and striking fear into the hearts of big league pitchers.

POSITION: FIRST BASE
BATS: RIGHT
THROWS: RIGHT
HT/WT: 6'3", 245 LB.
DEBUT: 3-28-19
TEAM: NEW YORK METS
BORN: 12-7-94, TAMPA, FL

AVG	OBP	SLG	OPS+	HR	RBI
.261	.349	.535	140	146	380

Yordan Álvarez

A native of Cuba, Yordan Álvarez emerged as a breakout talent as a 17-year-old and, almost immediately thereafter, defected to the United States and signed with the Los Angeles Dodgers. Less than two months after he was signed–and before he could play a single game as a professional–the Dodgers traded him to the Houston Astros for veteran reliever Josh Fields. According to some reports, the Dodgers thought the Astros were asking for minor league pitcher *Yadier* Álvarez, not Yordan, and mistakenly sent the latter along in the trade. Whether or not that's actually what happened, the deal will likely go down as one of the most lopsided trades in recent baseball history, as *Yordan* Álvarez would quickly become one of the most feared hitters in the game.

Álvarez made his professional debut in 2016 with the Dominican Summer League Astros, where he hit .341 with a .974 OPS in 16 games. In 2017 he played 90 total games across two levels of A-ball, hitting .304/.379/.481 with 12 home runs and 69 RBI in 335 at bats, earning a spot in the 2017 All-Star Futures Game. He split the 2018 season between the Double-A Corpus Christi and the Triple-A Fresno Grizzlies, hitting a combined .293/.369/.534/.904 with 63 runs, 20 home runs, and 74 RBI in 335 at bats. Álvarez opened the 2019 season in Triple-A once again, hitting .343/.443/.742 with 50 runs, 38 walks, 23 home runs, 71 RBIs, and an OPS of 1.185 in 213 at bats, leading the minor leagues in home runs, RBI, and total bases.

It was clear by now that Álvarez was ready for the big leagues, and he proved it by dominating at that level in 2019, batting .313/.412/.655 with 27 home runs and 75 RBI and becoming the unanimous winner of the AL Rookie of the Year Award. That year Álvarez's .655 slugging percentage and 1.067 OPS were both the highest in history for a rookie, exceeding the previous mark set by Shoeless Joe Jackson in 1911. After missing almost the entirety of the 2020 season due to knee surgery, Álvarez hit 33 homers and drove in 104 in 2021, helping lead the Astros to the World Series for the second time in three seasons. In 2022 he put up his strongest season to date, hitting .306/.406/.613 (187 OPS+) while leading the 106-win Astros in virtually every offensive category.

During the season Álvarez signed a six-year $115 million contract extension. Josh Fields, while having a couple of nice seasons for the Dodgers, retired following the 2018 season. I think it's safe to say that the Astros got the best out of that trade.

POSITION: OUTFIELD/DESIGNATED HITTER
BATS: LEFT
THROWS: RIGHT
HT/WT: 6'5", 225 LB.
DEBUT: 6-9-19
TEAM: HOUSTON ASTROS
BORN: 6-27-97, VICTORIA DE LAS TUNAS, LAS TUNAS PROVINCE, CUBA

AVG	OBP	SLG	OPS+	HR	RBI
.296	.384	.590	163	98	283

Tim Anderson

Tim Anderson was a basketball standout in Alabama but, once he stopped growing at 6'1", he decided that baseball–the other sport at which he excelled–was the way to go. It was a good choice. After two years of dominating play at Mississippi's East Central Community College, he pushed his way onto the big league scouting radar and was selected by the White Sox in the first round of the 2013 draft.

Anderson is not a perfect player. He makes more than his fair share of errors at shortstop, and he doesn't walk as much as many star players do. But he has a strong arm from the hole at short, and he has quick hands and the ability to hit to all fields with power. That combination compensates for the few shortcomings in his game. It compensates so well, in fact, that he has earned two All-Star Game appearances, a batting title, and a Silver Slugger Award over the course of his seven-year big league career.

His third year in the majors was when Anderson truly started to shine. In 2018 he used a great first month in which he hit .381 with six homers and 17 RBI in 22 games as a springboard for a .335/.357/.508 season which earned him that year's batting crown. In the pandemic-shortened 2020 season he played in 49 games, leading the AL with 45 runs scored while batting .322/.357/.529 en route to a Silver Slugger Award and a seventh-place finish in the race for MVP. The White Sox made it to the postseason for the first time in 12 years that season and, while the Sox bowed out in the first round, Anderson had nine hits in 14 at bats. In 2021, he was named an All-Star for the first time as the White Sox ran away with the AL Central title, thanks in large part to Anderson's contributions and leadership. A highlight came when he was the hero of the "Field of Dreams Game" played in a temporary ballpark erected in an Iowa cornfield. There, with the White Sox trailing the Yankees 8–7 in the bottom of the ninth, Anderson hit a two-run game-ending homer into the corn growing beyond the outfield to give Chicago the victory. He finished the season with an average of .309 in 123 games with 17 homers, 94 runs, and 61 RBI for an OPS+ of 118. He once again starred in the postseason, going 7 for 19 with 4 runs scored in a Division Series loss to the eventual AL champion Houston Astros.

Anderson started off 2022 on fire, but a hand injury in the middle of the season cut him short. He'll be back to full health in 2023, however, and should be at the top of the American League leaderboard for years to come.

POSITION: SHORTSTOP
BATS: RIGHT
THROWS: RIGHT
HT/WT: 6'1", 185 LB.
DEBUT: 6-10-16
TEAM: CHICAGO WHITE SOX
BORN: 6-23-93, TUSCALOOSA, AL

AVG	OBP	SLG	OPS+	HR	RBI
.288	.316	.442	105	97	313

Nolan Arenado

The Gold Glove has long been the, pardon the expression, gold standard for defensive excellence. One player at each position in each league wins a Gold Glove each year. Nolan Arenado has had a lock on that among National League third baseman during the course of his career, winning it an astounding 10 times in his 10 years as a big leaguer. That ties him with Mike Schmidt, who won 10 Gold Gloves in an 18-year career, and those two trail only Brooks Robinson who won 16 Gold Gloves in 23 seasons.

But have you ever heard of the Platinum Glove Award? That honor, invented in 2011, is given to the best defensive player of the year from each league, *regardless of position*. It is thus the most prestigious defensive award in baseball. Winning it means that you are the best, even compared to all of the other Gold Glovers. Well, Arenado has won the Platinum Glove Award *five times*. That mark, those 10 Gold Gloves, and what we've all been able to see with our own eyes over the course of his 10-year big league career, suggest that Arenado is one of the top defenders at any position ever.

Arenado would be an elite player if he were only a gloveman, but he's far from just that. He's also one of the top offensive players in the game. He's a seven-time All-Star, a four-time Silver Slug-ger winner, and has led the National League in home runs three times while leading all of Major League Baseball in RBI twice. Over the course of his career he has compiled a batting line of .289/.346/.535. While eight of those seasons were played for the Colorado Rockies—whose players tend to have inflated offensive numbers due to home games in the thin air of mile-high Coors Field in Denver—Arenado's 2022 season with the St. Louis Cardinals was clearly his best year yet. Arenado just keeps getting better.

One day Nolan Arenado is going to be elected to the Hall of Fame. The only question now is whether, when that happens, he will be *one* of the greatest third basemen in the game's history or *the absolute greatest* third baseman in history.

POSITION: THIRD BASE
BATS: RIGHT
THROWS: RIGHT
HT/WT: 6'2", 215 LB.
DEBUT: 4-28-13
TEAMS: COLORADO ROCKIES (2013–20), ST. LOUIS CARDINALS (2021–)
BORN: 4-16-91, NEWPORT BEACH, CA

AVG	OBP	SLG	OPS+	HR	RBI
.289	.346	.535	124	299	968

18

Mookie Betts can simply do it all. He hits for average and for power. He's a fast base runner and a smart base runner. He also plays an outstanding right field. He's even a professional-level bowler who has rolled at least three perfect games.

Heavily recruited for both baseball and basketball, Betts bypassed college when the Boston Red Sox selected him in the fifth round of the 2011 draft as an infielder. Unlike a lot of players, Betts did better every time he was promoted up the minor league ladder, seemingly preferring the tougher competition in the upper levels. Betts earned his first shot at the big leagues in 2014. And he performed well as a rookie, hitting .291 with five home runs in 52 games while playing in the outfield—rather than as an infielder—more than half the time. In 2015 he'd be the team's regular center fielder before moving permanently to right field in 2016.

It was around that time that Betts went from promising talent to full-blown superstar. In 2016 he finished the season with a .318 batting average, 214 hits, 122 runs scored, 42 doubles, 31 home runs, 113 RBI, and an MLB-leading 359 total bases while winning a Gold Glove, the Silver Slugger Award, and coming in second in MVP voting. Following a small step back in 2017—which still saw him win a Gold Glove and make the All-Star team—Betts put together a monster season in 2018. That year he hit an outstanding .346/.438/.640 with 32 homers and 30 stolen bases while becoming the first player in major league history to win the Most Valuable Player Award, the Silver Slugger Award, a Gold Glove, the batting title, and be on the World Series–winning team in the same season.

In 2019 Betts was awarded his fourth consecutive Gold Glove and his third Silver Slugger. It would prove to be his last season in Boston, however, as he was sent to the Dodgers in a trade that off-season. The change of scenery served him well, when he gave yet another fantastic campaign, hitting .292/.366/.562 with 47 runs, 16 home runs, 39 RBI, and stealing 10 bases in the pandemic-shortened season. That October, Betts won his second World Series ring. Given his track record, there will likely be more in his future.

POSITION: OUTFIELD
BATS: RIGHT
THROWS: RIGHT
HT/WT: 5'9", 180 LB.
DEBUT: 6-29-14
TEAMS: BOSTON RED SOX (2014–19), LOS ANGELES DODGERS (2020–)
BORN: 10-7-92, BRENTWOOD, TN

AVG	OBP	SLG	OPS+	HR	RBI
.293	.368	.520	134	213	649

Gerrit Cole

Pitching in the twenty-first century has been defined by velocity, strikeouts, and how much spin a pitcher can put on a baseball. By those measures, Gerrit Cole may be the archetypal pitcher of his era. He throws harder than almost everyone else, strikes out more batters than almost anyone else, and puts the sort of spin on a ball that makes his stuff harder to hit than almost anyone else's. He's a workhorse with an elite fastball, a pair of swing-and-miss secondary pitches, and the command over his pitches and strategic intelligence to maximize the utility of all of his physical gifts.

Cole was one of the top prep pitchers in the country, making the All-USA high school baseball team. Rather than sign with a big league club, however, Cole went to UCLA, where he led the Bruins to the best record in the school's history and a runner-up finish in the 2010 College World Series. The Pittsburgh Pirates selected Cole with the first overall pick of the 2011 draft, and he made his way to the big leagues by June of 2013. Cole finished that regular season with a 10–7 record and a 3.22 ERA in 19 starts and started Games Two and Five of the 2013 National League Division Series. He'd end up pitching for the Pirates for five seasons–winning 19 games and making the All-Star team in 2015, and leading the National League in starts while tossing 203 innings and striking out 196 batters in 2017.

On January 13, 2018, Cole was traded to Houston, where he took his game to the next level. He would finish his first season in Houston with a new career high of 278 strikeouts, a 15–5 record, and a 2.88 ERA, each of which were his best since 2015. He dominated against Cleveland in Game Two of the 2018 American League Division Series, striking out 12 and walking none in seven innings in a 3–1 victory. In doing so Cole became the second pitcher to strike out at least 12 hitters with no walks in the postseason, after Tom Seaver did it in 1973. Cole became a 20-game winner for the first time in 2019, while leading the league in ERA (2.50) and strikeouts (326) and striking out an outstanding 13.6 batters per nine innings. Cole set an MLB record late that season by pitching nine consecutive outings with at least 10 strikeouts.

On December 18, 2019, the New York Yankees signed Cole to a franchise record nine-year, $324 million contract. One-third of the way into that deal Cole has a record of 130–71 and continues to strike out batters at a high rate. Power pitchers like him tend to age well, so expect more of the same in the coming years.

POSITION: STARTING PITCHER
BATS: RIGHT
THROWS: RIGHT
HT/WT: 6'4", 220 LB.
DEBUT: 6-11-13
TEAMS: PITTSBURGH PIRATES (2013–17), HOUSTON ASTROS (2018–19), NEW YORK YANKEES (2020–)
BORN: 9-8-90, NEWPORT BEACH, CA

W	L	ERA	ERA+	IP	K	BB
130	71	3.23	127	1650	1930	423

Jacob deGrom

Jacob deGrom never planned on being a pitcher. In high school he was a star basketball player, and when he joined the Stetson University baseball team, he was an infielder. It wasn't until his junior year, when Stetson had him pitch a little bit, that scouts began to take note of his potential. The Mets took him in the ninth round of the 2010 draft. His track record and his draft position suggested that, at that point, the Mets considered him a project that might not make it. Boy, has he ever made it.

Things didn't look too promising at first as deGrom required reconstructive elbow surgery almost immediately on his minor league journey. He was healthy again by 2012, however, and began using his size and power to make some career headway. He won six of his 15 games for low-A Savannah, issuing just 14 walks in 89.2 innings, and continued that level of performance for the high-A St. Lucie Mets, posting an ERA of 2.08 and walking only 20 batters in 111.1 innings. DeGrom spent the 2013 season between St. Lucie, the Double-A Binghamton Triplets, and the Triple-A Las Vegas 51s, suffering a bit statistically speaking, but developing his overall approach—and his outstanding fastball velocity—in such a way that his big league call-up would be inevitable. That opportunity came in May of 2014, at which point deGrom put up a Rookie of the Year campaign thanks in large part to an impressive strikeout rate. But Mets fans and opponents hadn't seen anything yet.

DeGrom improved in each subsequent season, making the All-Star team in 2015 and, after battling through some injuries in 2016, setting career highs for innings and strikeouts the following year. He put it all together in 2018, winning the Cy Young Award on the back of a 1.70 ERA and 269 strikeouts while allowing just 10 homers and lighting up the radar gun to triple digits on multiple occasions. In 2019 he did it again, winning his second Cy Young in a row while leading the league in punch-outs thanks to an even faster fastball than he had featured the year before, and the development of his slider into, arguably, the hardest to hit pitch in all of baseball.

DeGrom's 2021 and 2022 campaigns were thrilling and frustrating by turns. Thrilling insofar as, when he did pitch, he threw harder and more effectively than any starting pitcher has in some time. Frustrating in terms of nagging injuries limiting him to only 15 starts in 2021 and 11 in 2022. So far those aches and pains have not diminished his quality, however, and there remains every reason to believe that more triple-digit heaters—and maybe another Cy Young—are in his future.

POSITION: STARTING PITCHER
BATS: LEFT · **THROWS:** RIGHT
HT/WT: 6'4", 180 LB.
DEBUT: 5-15-14
TEAM: NEW YORK METS
BORN: 6-19-88, DELAND, FL

W	L	ERA	ERA+	IP	K	BB
82	57	2.52	155	1326	1607	303

Edwin Díaz

It's the top of the ninth inning and the New York Mets are holding on to a slim lead. Suddenly, the lights of Citi Field dim, and a propulsive drumbeat begins to pound through the stadium's speakers, eventually making way for a glorious trumpet solo to fill the ballpark. The bullpen doors open, the crowd cheers wildly, and in runs closer Edwin Díaz, poised to lock down yet another Mets victory. That was the scene for most of the 2022 season as Díaz dominated in the late innings, while helping the Mets make the postseason for the first time in six years.

Díaz began his career with the Seattle Mariners, who drafted him in the third round of the 2012 amateur draft out of Caguas Military Academy in Puerto Rico. By 2015 he had worked his way up to Double-A and a spot on the World team for that year's Futures Game. By 2016 he was the Mariners' number two prospect. Seattle converted him from a starter into a relief pitcher that year so he might more readily fill a need at the big league level. He was called up in early June and made his debut by pitching a scoreless inning against Cleveland, a game in which he hit 101 mph on the radar gun. By early August Seattle had named Díaz the team's everyday closer, and he excelled in the role, picking up 18 saves before the season was out, posting an excellent 2.79 ERA, and striking out 88 batters in 51.2 innings over 49 appearances.

Díaz returned as the M's closer in 2017 and added another 34 saves to his record while continuing to strike out batters at a healthy clip. He took things up a whole other level in 2018, though, becoming almost untouchable en route

to a 57-save season, which was and remains the second highest total in a single season by any pitcher. Díaz also struck out 124 batters and issued just 17 walks in 73.1 innings while posting a 1.96 ERA and winning the Mariano Rivera Award as the best relief pitcher in the American League.

Díaz was traded to New York following the season and, at first, he struggled with the Mets. An early season contract dispute started the year off wrong, and Díaz could never find his footing on the mound. He was relieved of his closer role during the 2019 campaign and his future looked questionable, but he bounced back to his All-Star form in 2020 and continued that way in 2021 before returning to the top of the relief pitcher pyramid in 2022.

Relief pitchers' careers can be unpredictable. Today's top dogs could find themselves out of a job in a year, and last season's nobody could just as easily be this season's star. Edwin Díaz has seen both the ups and the downs of ninth inning work. Given how thoroughly he's been embraced by Mets fans, there are a lot of people who hope the current ups last a good long while.

POSITION: RELIEF PITCHER
BATS: RIGHT
THROWS: RIGHT
HT/WT: 6'3", 165 LB.
DEBUT: 6-6-16
TEAMS: SEATTLE MARINERS (2016–18),
  NEW YORK METS (2019–)
BORN: 3-22-94, NAGUABO, PR

W	L	ERA	ERA+	IP	K	BB
16	29	2.93	139	399.1	657	141

Freddie Freeman

There are few hitters in Major League Baseball who are more consistent year in and year out than Freddie Freeman. Since almost the moment he debuted, he has hit for average and for power in equal measure and is one of the best in the game at beating defensive shifts, thereby making him hard to neutralize. He's done all of this while playing a top-caliber first base, making Freeman one of the best all-around players in the game.

Freeman was a third baseman and a pitcher at El Modena High School in Orange, California, and after an outstanding prep career, he was offered a scholarship to powerhouse Cal State Fullerton. When the Atlanta Braves selected Freeman in the second round of the 2007 draft, however, Freeman put college on hold and set out on his professional career. While not originally considered a can't-miss prospect, Freeman slowly climbed the ladder of the minor league rankings and made himself a top-15 overall prospect by the end of the 2009 season. He'd finally make the big club as a September call-up in 2010 and would begin the 2011 season as the Braves' starting first baseman.

After a slow start, Freeman established himself as one of the top rookies in the game. He became the first Braves rookie to reach 50 RBI by the All-Star break since Hank Aaron accomplished the feat in 1954 and was named NL Rookie of the Month for July. Freeman finished the 2011 season batting .282 with 32 doubles, 21 home runs, and 76 RBI in 157 games played, coming in second to teammate Craig Kimbrel in the NL Rookie of the Year balloting.

After a minor step back in 2012, Freeman took his game to the next level in 2013 and began a stretch of outstanding seasons that continues to this day. Between 2013 and 2021, Freeman hit .302/.394/.523 and averaged 25 homers and 33 doubles a year. During that stretch he made the All-Star team five times, won a Gold Glove in 2018 and the Silver Slugger Award three times. His best season came in the pandemic-shortened 2020 campaign when Freeman won the NL MVP Award while batting .341/.462/.640 and leading the league in runs scored and doubles. The following season he was the leader of an Atlanta Braves team which won the World Series, upsetting both the powerful Los Angeles Dodgers and the Houston Astros in the process. In Game Five of the Series Freeman hit a home run that traveled 460 feet, and he recorded the final putout of Game Six, ending the Series.

Freeman became a free agent following the World Series and signed a six-year, $162 million contract with the Dodgers, who play only a few miles from where he grew up and starred as a high schooler. In his first season with the Dodgers he picked up right where he left off with Atlanta, leading the league in batting, on-base percentage, runs scored, hits, and doubles.

Freddie Freeman is a machine. Wind him up, point him toward the batter's box, and watch him go.

POSITION: FIRST BASE
BATS: LEFT • **THROWS:** RIGHT
HT/WT: 6'5", 220 LB.
DEBUT: 9-1-10
TEAMS: ATLANTA BRAVES (2010–21); LOS ANGELES DODGERS (2022–)
BORN: 9-12-89, VILLA PARK, CA

AVG	OBP	SLG	OPS+	HR	RBI
.298	.386	.509	140	292	1041

Paul Goldschmidt

In baseball terms, age 35 is around the time when careers tend to wind down. But that certainly wasn't the case for St. Louis Cardinals first baseman Paul Goldschmidt. He turned 35 in 2022 and managed to complete the finest season in his 12-year career. He batted .317/.404/.578 (OPS+ 180) and led the Cardinals to yet another National League Central title. But though it was his best year, 2022 was not some crazy outlier. Goldschmidt has been one of the game's top offensive performers for his entire career.

Goldschmidt won a state championship as a high schooler out of The Woodlands, Texas, in 2006, and then went on to play for Texas State University, where he continued to shine. He was named the Southland Conference Hitter of the Year in 2008 and 2009, Southland Player of the Year in 2009, and was a third-team All-American as a junior in 2009 after hitting .352 with 18 home runs and 88 runs batted in just 57 games. He went on to be selected in the eighth round of the 2009 draft. He made his major league debut with the Arizona Diamondbacks on August 1, 2011.

By his second full season Goldschmidt would lead the National League in home runs, RBI, slugging percentage, and OPS+ while also picking up a Gold Glove at first base and the 2013 Silver Slugger Award for first basemen. He's made six more All-Star teams since then while averaging 32 homers and 104 RBI for every 162 games played. He's earned MVP votes in nine of his 12 seasons in the majors.

The key to Goldschmidt's performance is that he basically has no weaknesses at the plate. According to advanced statistical measures, he is an above-average hitter against every pitch you can name, be they fastballs, sliders, curveballs, cutters, or changeups, and he is more or less equally good against right-handed and left-handed pitchers. That's a rare quality in most hitters, but it's especially rare in a power hitter like Goldschmidt.

There aren't a lot of players whose best seasons have come when they were in their mid-30s. Those that have experienced this continue playing at a high level for several more years after that. If that's true for Goldschmidt, the Hall of Fame will almost certainly be in his future.

POSITION: FIRST BASE
BATS: RIGHT
THROWS: RIGHT
HT/WT: 6'3", 220 LB.
DEBUT: 8-1-11
TEAMS: ARIZONA DIAMONDBACKS (2011–18), ST. LOUIS CARDINALS (2019–)
BORN: 9-10-87, WILMINGTON, DE

AVG	OBP	SLG	OPS+	HR	RBI
.295	.391	.527	145	315	1042

Vladimir Guerrero Jr.

The son of Hall of Famer Vladimir Guerrero, Vlad Jr. also began impressing talent evaluators when he was a teenager, tagging along with his dad to batting practice. Former Blue Jays general manager Alex Anthopoulos recalls seeing him launching homers over a major league fence when he was just 14 years old and made a point to sign him the moment he was old enough to put his name on a contract. Between his father's imposing legacy and his youthful promise, expectations for Guerrero were high, and the pressure placed on him at such a young age was unprecedented. Still, he has met those expectations and has thus far fulfilled that promise.

Guerrero has made a habit of doing great things way before most people his age have managed to make a mark. He hit his first home run when he was only 17, playing in the Appalachian League, where most players are over 20. He was the youngest player ever named to the Futures Game, which showcases the top minor league talent in the world. He became the first minor leaguer to receive a perfect score of 80 on the major league scouting scale for his overall hitting ability, which is something only the top superstars in the game ever achieve.

Promise counts for little once a player faces big league pitching, of course, but Guerrero has lived up to the hype. In his first two campaigns–2019 and the pandemic-shortened 2020 season–Guerrero hit 24 homers and drove in 102 runs over 183 games despite being younger than almost every player in baseball. He made big headlines during the 2019 All-Star break when, despite being a rookie with only eight homers to his credit at that point, he competed in the Home Run Derby, hitting a record 29 homers in the first round, then 40 in the second round before falling just one short of eventual winner Pete Alonso in the finals. His 91 homers overall shattered the previous derby record.

In 2021, when he was 22, Guerrero put it all together and truly broke out, leading the league in home runs (48), runs (123), on-base percentage (.401), slugging percentage (.602), OPS (1.002), OPS+ (167), and total bases (363). He finished second in the MVP Award voting that year behind Shohei Ohtani. In 2022 he once again starred, making the All-Star team and helping power the Blue Jays to the postseason for the second time in his four seasons as a major leaguer.

POSITION: FIRST BASE
BATS: RIGHT
THROWS: RIGHT
HT/WT: 6'2", 240 LB.
DEBUT: 4-26-19
TEAM: TORONTO BLUE JAYS
BORN: 3-16-99, MONTREAL, QC, CANADA

AVG	OBP	SLG	OPS+	HR	RBI
.284	.358	.504	135	104	310

Bryce Harper

Bryce Harper appeared on the cover of *Sports Illustrated* in June 2009 when he was just 16, next to the words "Baseball's Chosen One," and was referred to in the article as "the most exciting prodigy since LeBron." Still just a high school sophomore, he was named *Baseball America*'s High School Player of the Year that year, but he dropped out of school to get his GED so he could become eligible for the 2010, draft rather than wait until 2011 when players in what would've been his graduating class could've been selected. In the meantime he spent a season playing for the College of Southern Nevada where, at age 17, he broke the school's home run record, was named the conference player of the year, and was the recipient of the 2010 Golden Spikes Award honoring the best college baseball player in the United States.

It's impossible to overstate the fanfare that accompanied Harper's every move in those days, and when the Washington Nationals made him the number one overall selection in the 2010 draft, expectations were sky high. Harper was named *Baseball's America*'s number one prospect before he had played his first true minor league game and justified that honor, excelling in two minor league divisions where he was three or four years younger than most of his competition. In 2012 he began the season at Triple-A–again, where most players were considerably older than he was–but was called up to the majors in April due to injuries on the big club. He hasn't looked back since.

Harper made the All-Star team and was the NL Rookie of the year in 2012. In 2013 he was voted an All-Star Game starter, making him the youngest National League player to ever receive that honor. A thumb injury disrupted his 2014 campaign, but in 2015 he dominated the game, hitting .330/.460/.639 while smacking 42 homers and winning the MVP Award via unanimous vote at just 22. After reaching free agency following the 2018 season, Harper signed a 13-year, $330 million contract with the Philadelphia Phillies, which at the time was the largest contract in baseball history. Harper won another MVP Award in 2021, batting .309/.429/.615 and leading the league with 42 home runs.

Harper has been in the public eye for so long it's amazing that he just turned 30 following the 2022 season. But despite his age, he has already compiled a résumé which is pushing him into Hall of Fame territory. With nine more years left on his contract with the Phillies–and many years until he's at the age when most great players retire–the sky remains the limit for one of baseball's most talked-about talents.

POSITION: OUTFIELD/DESIGNATED HITTER
BATS: LEFT
THROWS: RIGHT
HT/WT: 6'3", 210 LB.
DEBUT: 4-28-12
TEAMS: WASHINGTON NATIONALS (2012–18), PHILADELPHIA PHILLIES (2019–)
BORN: 10-16-92, LAS VEGAS, NV

| .280 | .390 | .523 | 142 | 285 | 817 |

Aaron Judge

Baseball is a cyclical game in which, for a few years at a time, pitchers will have the advantage over hitters. Then the dynamic will reverse and the hitters will reign supreme. The late teens and early 2020s, for example, have been a pitching-first era, with offense generally being depressed and pitchers dominant. Usually in such cases the league leaders in offense will sport lower home run totals and overall offensive numbers than the best hitters from more offensive-oriented eras. No one, however, appears to have told Aaron Judge that.

The Yankees outfielder put up a season for the ages in 2022, hitting 62 homers—a new American League record—in a year in which his next-closest competitor only managed 46. That, along with his .311/.425/.686 (OPS+ 211) season, stands as evidence that Judge is playing a different game than the competition in almost every way that matters. Not that 2022 was a tremendous fluke. Judge hit 52 homers and drove in 127 runs as a rookie in 2017 and has posted an OPS+ of 140 or more in every full season in which he's played. He has arguably the best raw power of any hitter in the game, and his strike zone judgment has improved considerably since he first broke into the big leagues.

Judge is unique in ways beyond just his performance, too. At 6 feet 7 inches, he is the tallest person in baseball history to have a 50-homer season, and he has done it twice. There haven't been many hitters of his physical stature overall. Usually baseball players his size become pitchers if they don't become football or basketball players first—each of which Judge had a good chance at thanks to his multisports acumen in high school. He bypassed offers in those sports in order to play baseball at Fresno State University, and when the Yankees took him in the first round of the 2013 draft, that decision paid off handsomely.

Judge's judgment has always been pretty good in that regard, actually. Prior to the 2022 season, the Yankees made him a contract extension offer reportedly worth $213 million. It was a lot of money to be sure, but Judge chose instead to start the final season before he reached free agency—betting on himself and believing that he could put up a strong enough season that the contract he eventually signed would be much larger. With his historic 62, that bet paid off too.

POSITION: OUTFIELD
BATS: RIGHT
THROWS: RIGHT
HT/WT: 6'7", 282 LB.
DEBUT: 8-13-16
TEAM: NEW YORK YANKEES
BORN: 4-26-92, LINDEN, CA

AVG	OBP	SLG	OPS+	HR	RBI
.284	.394	.583	163	220	497

Manny Machado

It was clear from a very young age that Manny Machado would be a superstar. Growing up in a hotbed of baseball talent in South Florida, Machado was on scouts' radar early on and was drafted by the Baltimore Orioles with the third overall pick in 2010, just before his 18th birthday.

Machado would require less than two full seasons in the minor leagues before making his major league debut in August 2012. He'd break out as a star in his first full big league season, 2013, earning a spot on the American League All-Star team while leading the league in doubles with 51 and at bats with 657 while winning a Gold Glove Award. Though an injury cut his 2014 season short, beginning in 2015 and continuing to this day, Machado has been one of the most durable and reliable players in baseball, never playing fewer than 150 games in a season, not counting the pandemic-shortened 2020 campaign.

Machado has been the portrait of consistency over the course of his career, both as a hitter and with the glove. He won his second Gold Glove in 2015, and made the All-Star team in 2015, 2016, 2018, and 2022. He's hit more than 30 homers in six of his 11 big league seasons and has driven in over 100 runs three times. It's the sort of production that teams would love to get from a first baseman or corner outfielder, but it's come from a guy who has played an outstanding defensive third base and a little bit of shortstop over the course of his career.

It's production that has made Machado highly sought-after as well. In 2018, as an impending free agent on an Orioles team that was not in the playoff hunt, Machado was traded to the Los Angeles Dodgers and helped the team reach the World Series. That off-season, Machado signed a 10-year, $300 million contract with the Padres which, at the time, was the richest contract in the history of North American sports. Since then, Machado has become a team leader on the Padres, taking that club's young talent under his wing. That paid off in a postseason appearance in 2022. There will likely be many more before Machado's career is over.

POSITION: THIRD BASE
BATS: RIGHT
THROWS: RIGHT
HT/WT: 6'3", 218 LB.
DEBUT: 8-9-12
TEAMS: BALTIMORE ORIOLES (2012–18),
  LOS ANGELES DODGERS (2018),
  SAN DIEGO PADRES (2019–)
BORN: 7-6-92, MIAMI, FL

AVG	OBP	SLG	OPS+	HR	RBI
.282	.341	.493	126	283	853

Shohei Ohtani

There are great hitters and there are great pitchers. Since Shohei Ohtani made his major league debut in 2018, however, he has become the first player to dominate both as a hitter *and* as a pitcher since the great Babe Ruth did so over a century ago.

As a high schooler in Iwate Prefecture, Japan, Ohtani's fastball was already being clocked at 99 mph, and his 6'4" frame gave him imposing power as a hitter. While almost all young players in both the United States and Japan are forced to choose either pitching or hitting once they turn pro, the team that drafted Ohtani out of high school–the Hokkaido Nippon-Ham Fighters–allowed him to do both. By his third season, in 2015, he was leading all of Japanese baseball with a 2.24 ERA. The following year his ERA improved to 1.86, and he smacked 22 homers while leading the Fighters to Pacific League and Japan Series championships. In 2017 he decided he wanted to play in the United States, and after being courted by all 30 MLB clubs, Ohtani agreed to a deal with the Los Angeles Angels.

Despite enormous pressure–from both the high expectations of fans and intense media coverage–Ohtani hit .285 with 22 home runs while also posting a 3.31 ERA in 10 games as a starting pitcher in 2018, earning the American League Rookie of the Year Award. Due to elbow surgery following that season, Ohtani only batted for all of 2019 and most of the 2020 season, and many people thought he should ditch pitching and concentrate on his offense. He returned as a two-way player in 2021, however, and dominated both sides of the game. That year he hit 46 home runs and drove in 100 as a designated hitter while starting 23 games as a pitcher and posting a 3.18 ERA with 156 strikeouts in 130.1 innings. He was named an All-Star at both positions and was the unanimous choice as the American League's Most Valuable Player. Ohtani's pitching actually improved in 2022 while he continued to be one of the game's foremost power hitters.

There is simply no other player in all of baseball like Shohei Ohtani. In all likelihood, there won't be another like him for a very, very long time.

POSITION: STARTING PITCHER/ DESIGNATED HITTER
BATS: LEFT
THROWS: RIGHT
HT/WT: 6'4", 210 LB.
DEBUT: 3-29-18
TEAM: LOS ANGELES ANGELS
BORN: 7-5-94, OSHU, IWATE PREFECTURE, JAPAN

AVG	OBP	SLG	OPS+	HR	RBI
.267	.354	.532	139	127	342

W	L	ERA	ERA+	IP	K	BB
28	14	2.96	142	349.2	441	118

José Ramírez

There are few major league superstars whose ascension to stardom was more improbable than José Ramírez's.

Ramírez signed out of the Dominican Republic for very little money, due primarily to his size—he's only 5'9"—and a set of skills that suggested he would top out as a utility infielder. His ability to make contact early in his minor league career suggested that he'd be a *very good* utility infielder, of course, but no one figured he'd become a perennial MVP candidate. Somewhere along the line, however, Ramírez managed to master a swing that puts the barrel on the ball and sends it in the air in ways that don't make a ton of sense for someone with his size and his mechanics. Still, he somehow learned to generate power from both sides of the plate all the same while continuing to be a solid contact hitter. By his fourth year in the majors he was a key part of Cleveland's 2016 AL Pennant–winning team and even got a few MVP votes thrown his way following the season.

Ramírez truly broke out as a star in 2017 when he hit an astonishing 56 doubles to lead all of baseball, made the All-Star team, won a Silver Slugger Award, and finished third in the MVP balloting thanks to a .318/.374/.583 campaign. He continued to swing a hot bat in 2018, landing himself a spot on the All-Star team and a third-place finish in the MVP voting for the second straight year. Following an uncharacteristic off-year in 2019, Ramírez has put up three straight seasons of top production, combining to hit .276/.360/.539 (148 OPS+) between 2020 and 2022 while picking up another Silver Slugger Award, a second place MVP finish in 2020, and All-Star selections in 2021 and 2022.

Maybe the thing that endears him most to Cleveland Guardians fans, however, is that he truly loves to play in the city. That became clear when, on April 6, 2022, Ramírez signed a five-year, $124 million extension which will keep him with the club through 2028. The deal includes a full no-trade clause, and when Ramírez appeared at the press conference announcing the deal, he said that since Cleveland believed in him when no one else thought too highly of him he cannot imagine playing for anyone else.

POSITION: THIRD BASE
BATS: BOTH
THROWS: RIGHT
HT/WT: 5'9", 190 LB.
DEBUT: 9-1-13
TEAM: CLEVELAND GUARDIANS
BORN: 9-17-92, BANÍ, PERAVIA PROVINCE, DOMINICAN REPUBLIC

AVG	OBP	SLG	OPS+	HR	RBI
.279	.354	.503	129	192	666

Austin Riley

A combination baseball/football prospect out of DeSoto County, Mississippi, Austin Riley had his choice of sports when Mississippi State University offered him a dual scholarship. When the Atlanta Braves selected Riley in the first round of the 2015 draft, however, he put school on hold to start his professional career.

While his rise through the bush leagues was not as meteoric as the ascent of some other players, he hit 67 home runs in his three and a half minor league seasons. Riley was called up to Atlanta on May 15, 2019, debuting in the outfield instead of his traditional third base. He got off to a scorching hot start, being named the May 2019 Rookie of the Month despite playing in only 15 games. He'd cool off the rest of the way in 2019 and would struggle some in the pandemic-shortened 2020 season, but broke out as a superstar in 2021.

That year Riley—now ensconced at his usual third base—batted .303 with 33 homers and 107 RBI while playing 160 games. Riley won the Silver Slugger Award as the best-hitting third baseman in the league and finished seventh in the voting for the MVP. He was also a huge post-season contributor, hitting .333 in that year's Division Series against the Milwaukee Brewers and .320 in the Braves World Series victory over the Houston Astros.

Riley continued to be Atlanta's top offensive contributor in 2022 and, on August 1 of that season, he signed a 10-year contract extension worth $212 million. That's the biggest contract in team history and assures that he will be the heart and soul of the Braves lineup for years to come.

POSITION: THIRD BASE
BATS: RIGHT
THROWS: RIGHT
HT/WT: 6'3", 240 LB.
DEBUT: 5-15-19
TEAM: ATLANTA BRAVES
BORN: 4-2-97, MEMPHIS, TN

AVG	OBP	SLG	OPS+	HR	RBI
.272	.339	.507	123	97	276

Julio Rodríguez

Though he has only one major league season under his belt, Julio Rodríguez has already established himself as the brightest star for Seattle Mariners fans to cheer for in many, many years, and as one of the top young talents in the game.

Signed out of the Dominican Republic in 2018, Rodríguez made short work of the minor leagues, dominating the Dominican Summer League that year. In 2019 he continued to excel in the U.S.-based minors, hitting .293/.359/.490 with 20 doubles, 50 runs, and 50 RBI in 67 games for West Virginia in the A-level South Atlantic League and .462/.514/.738 with 19 RBI and 13 runs in 17 games for Modesto of the California League. By the end of the season he found himself on *Baseball America's* top prospects lists, ranked as the number eight prospect in all of baseball entering 2020. Unfortunately, the 2020 minor league season was wiped out by the COVID-19 pandemic, though Rodríguez did play winter ball in the Dominican Republic. He ascended even higher on the prospect lists after outstanding play for High-A Arkansas and Double-A Everett in 2021, combining for a batting line of .347/.441/.560 with 13 homers and 21 stolen bases while also performing at a high level for the Dominican Republic national team.

In recent years, many teams have delayed calling up top minor league talent in an effort to save some money and retain contractual control over the player. While many assumed the Mariners would do the same, Rodríguez's talent proved undeniable, and after a strong 2022 spring training, he broke camp with Seattle and embarked on a truly outstanding rookie campaign.

He started slowly, batting .206 and slugging .260 in April, but on May 1 he blasted his first major league homer—a 450-foot bomb—while going 3 for 4 in a win over the Marlins. He was named the AL Rookie of the Month in May and won the honor again in June when he batted .280 with 7 homers, 16 RBI, and 22 runs scored. Those two months of work earned him a spot in the 2022 All-Star Game in which he also took part in the Home Run Derby, smacking 81 homers—more than anyone in the eight-man field—before losing the final round to Juan Soto. Later in the season he became only the fourth player to hit 20 homers and steal 20 bases in his rookie year.

On August 26, Rodríguez and the Mariners agreed on a huge 12-year contract extension, worth a guaranteed $210 million at a minimum, but which could reach up to $470 million. On September 30 his Mariners clinched their first playoff appearance in 21 years. They have Rodríguez to thank for that long-awaited success. And they'll have Rodríguez on the team for a very long time as they work to maintain it.

POSITION: OUTFIELD
BATS: RIGHT
THROWS: RIGHT
HT/WT: 6'3", 228 LB.
DEBUT: 4-8-22
TEAM: SEATTLE MARINERS
BORN: 12-29-00, LOMA DE CABRERA, DAJABÓN PROVINCE, DOMINICAN REPUBLIC

AVG	OBP	SLG	OPS+	HR	RBI
.284	.345	.509	147	28	75

Max Scherzer

Eventually, age catches up with every athlete. Max Scherzer will turn 39 in 2023 but, to date, there is no sign that he is anywhere close to slowing down.

After an exceptional career at the University of Missouri, Scherzer was the first round draft pick of the Arizona Diamondbacks in 2006 and had made his way to the majors by early 2008. Scherzer tossed four and a third perfect innings in his big league debut, striking out seven, and setting a major league record for the consecutive batters retired to begin his career (13). By 2009 he was the Diamondbacks fifth starter. Arizona did not, however, seem to appreciate what they had on their hands in Scherzer, and they packaged him in a massive, three-team trade with the Tigers and the Yankees following the season, which landed him in Detroit.

Between 2010 and 2012 Scherzer, comfortably ensconced in the Tigers rotation, steadily improved. His already amazing stuff had him racking up impressive strikeout totals and, eventually, he matched this to exceptional command and control and the sort of pitching IQ that only comes with experience. In 2012 he was a key part of the Tigers star-studded pennant-winning squad, and as the 2013 season dawned, Scherzer—by this time known as "Mad Max"—was poised to break out into superstardom. And break out he did.

That year Scherzer won the American League Cy Young Award, leading the league in wins (21) and winning percentage (.875) while allowing the fewest combined walks and hits per innings pitched in the AL. He once again led the league in wins in 2014, making his second consecutive All-Star team and coming in fifth in the Cy Young balloting. Scherzer became a free agent in the 2014–15 off-season and signed a massive contract with the Washington Nationals. He'd earn every penny of it and then some, winning two more Cy Young Awards—in 2016 and 2017—while leading the National League in wins in 2016 and 2018; in strikeouts in 2016, 2017, and 2018; and in strikeout-to-walk ratio four times in five seasons all while being the game's most durable starting pitcher. In 2019 he helped the Nationals win an improbable and career-capping World Series title. There were, it seemed, no more worlds left for Mad Max to conquer.

Except he hasn't stopped. Following an injury-hampered 2020 campaign, Scherzer continued his dominance in 2021, splitting time with Washington and the Los Angeles Dodgers, to which he was traded midseason and then helped reach the National League Championship Series. He signed with the New York Mets as a free agent prior to 2022 and, not surprisingly, helped lead them to the 2022 postseason while once again standing among the league leaders in multiple pitching categories.

At some point age will catch up with Max Scherzer—but not today.

POSITION: STARTING PITCHER
BATS: RIGHT · **THROWS:** RIGHT
HT/WT: 6'3", 208 LB.
DEBUT: 4-29-08
TEAMS: ARIZONA DIAMONDBACKS (2008–9), DETROIT TIGERS (2010–14), WASHINGTON NATIONALS (2015–21), LOS ANGELES DODGERS (2021), NEW YORK METS (2022–)
BORN: 7-27-84, ST. LOUIS, MO

W	L	ERA	ERA+	IP	K	BB
201	102	3.11	135	2682	3193	701

Corey Seager

Corey Seager's road to the majors was probably more familiar to him than to his fellow members of the 2012 draft class. That's because his brother Kyle, six years his senior, had already been in the big leagues for a year and a half by that point. It wasn't long, however, before Corey would surpass his older brother–an excellent player in his own right–to become one of the best players in the game.

A first-round pick of the Dodgers, Seager breezed through five levels of the minor leagues in just over three years, exhibiting a mature plate approach and ably handling the most important defensive position on the field: shortstop. He made a brief appearance in the big leagues at the end of the 2015 season and began the 2016 campaign as the Dodgers starting short-stop–their youngest Opening Day shortstop since 1944–and ranked as the top prospect in the game. He finished his rookie season with a .308 batting average, 26 home runs, and 72 RBI in 157 games and was named the National League Rookie of the Year.

Seager batted .295/.375/.479 with 22 home runs, was named to his second straight All-Star Game, and won his second consecutive Silver Slugger Award in 2017. He'd miss almost the entirety of the 2018 season due to elbow surgery but came back in 2019 to lead the National League in doubles and drive in 87 runs. In 2020 Seager played in 51 of his team's 60 games and hit .307/.358/.585, leading all Dodgers hitters in batting average, slugging percentage, hits, doubles, and RBI. That October he was named MVP of the National League Championship Series and MVP of the World Series, in which he hit .347/.439/.816 with 7 home runs and 16 RBI while leading the Dodgers to their first championship since 1988.

Following another outstanding campaign for the Dodgers in 2021, Seager entered the free agent market as the most highly sought-after shortstop in a very crowded free agent shortstop class. That fall he signed a 10-year, $325 million contract with the Texas Rangers, which stands as the largest deal in team history.

POSITION: SHORTSTOP
BATS: LEFT
THROWS: RIGHT
HT/WT: 6'4", 215 LB.
DEBUT: 9-3-15
TEAMS: LOS ANGELES DODGERS (2015–21), TEXAS RANGERS (2022–)
BORN: 4-27-94, CHARLOTTE, NC

AVG	OBP	SLG	OPS+	HR	RBI
.287	.357	.494	128	137	447

Juan Soto

Being compared to the great Ted Williams would be a lot, even for a seasoned veteran whose career had been on a Hall of Fame trajectory for years. For a player in his early 20s it's virtually unheard of. Juan Soto has garnered such comparisons, however, and it's not hard to see why.

Ever since he signed with the Washington Nationals as a 17-year-old, Soto has been lauded for his mature approach to hitting. He walks far more than he strikes out. He waits for the pitch he wants rather than being content with whatever the pitcher is offering. He uses all fields, and when he does take on a pitch, he swings with confidence and power. Soto is just 24 years old now, yet his discipline at the plate matches that of the most seasoned of veterans.

Soto made his big league debut in 2018, called up because of injuries on the big club but likewise earning the promotion by dominating in the minors. At the time he was the youngest player in the majors, but it didn't show in his performance as he hit an impressive .292/.406/.517 with 22 home runs in 116 games en route to a second place finish in the Rookie of the Year voting. He avoided a sophomore slump and then some in 2019, hitting .282/.401/.548 with 34 homers, 110 runs, and 110 RBI in 150 games while helping the Nationals overcome a poor start to make the postseason and upset both the Los Angeles Dodgers and the Houston Astros to win the World Series. In Game One of the Series, Soto became the fourth youngest player to hit a homer in the Fall Classic. In all he went 9 for 27 with two doubles and three homers, scoring six runs and driving in seven as the Nationals defeated the Astros in seven games.

Soto continued to be an offensive force over the next two years, leading the National League in hitting, on-base percentage, slugging percentage, OPS+, and intentional walks in 2020 and leading the league in free passes once again in 2021 while also pacing the circuit in walks and on-base percentage. The caution with which opposing pitchers treat him is a testament to how dangerous a hitter he is. In 2022 the Nationals, in the midst of a rebuild, traded Soto to the San Diego Padres. Soto struggled following the move, but having spurned a reported $440 million contract offer from Washington, he has clearly bet on himself. Based on everything he's accomplished so far, he's almost certain to win that bet.

POSITION: OUTFIELD
BATS: LEFT
THROWS: LEFT
HT/WT: 6'2", 224 LB.
DEBUT: 5-15-18
TEAMS: WASHINGTON NATIONALS (2018–22), SAN DIEGO PADRES (2022–)
BORN: 10-25-98, SANTO DOMINGO, DISTRITO NACIONAL, DOMINICAN REPUBLIC

AVG	OBP	SLG	OPS+	HR	RBI
.287	.424	.526	157	125	374

Fernando Tatís Jr.

Fernando Tatís Jr.'s father was a big leaguer who played 11 years in the majors and is the only player in major league history to hit two grand slams in one inning. That's the sort of thing that would almost always make you the most famous person in your family. Over the past four years, however, Fernando Tatís Sr.'s fame has been more than overtaken by that of his talented young son. Given that Junior is just getting started, that shadow is only going to grow longer.

Tatís was considered one of the top international prospects available when he signed his first professional contract with the White Sox in 2015, but for reasons they have long since come to regret, they traded him to the San Diego Padres for a veteran pitcher before he had a chance to play in his first professional game. By 2017, when he was still just 18 years old, Tatís moved up all the way to Double-A thanks to posting a .281/.390/.520 line in 117 games for the Fort Wayne Wizards of the Midwest League. He held his own in Double-A for the remainder of the season despite being a full six years younger than the average player in the league. Between both levels Tatís hit 27 doubles and 22 homers and drove in 75 runs, securing himself a place on all of baseball's top prospect lists.

By the beginning of 2019, Tatís was not only on those prospect lists—he ranked as one of the top three prospects in baseball. On March 26, 2019, the Padres surprised many when they announced that the 20-year-old Tatís had made the Opening Day roster. Despite missing a big chunk of the season due to a back injury, he finished it hitting .317/.379/.590 with 22 home runs, 61 runs, and 106 hits over 84 games. He came in third place in balloting for the National League Rookie of the Year Award that year, but everyone acknowledged that he was, by far, the top young talent in the game. In 2020 he batted .277/.366/.571, finishing second in runs scored, second in home runs, fourth in RBI, and fourth in stolen bases while also pacing the league in many more advanced statistical categories. In 2021 he took his game to an even higher level, leading the league with 42 home runs while improving his performance in virtually every offensive category, finishing third in the MVP voting and winning his second Silver Slugger Award.

Tatís missed the entire 2022 season, first because of a broken wrist and, later, because he was suspended for 80 games for using performance-enhancing drugs. The latter was a substantial blow to his reputation, and it will take a lot of work on his part to come back, both as a ballplayer and as one of the game's most marketable young stars. The hope is that Tatís will take the right lessons from his mistakes and resume the career path that, in his first three seasons, made him one of the brightest stars in the game.

POSITION: SHORTSTOP
BATS: RIGHT
THROWS: RIGHT
HT/WT: 6'3", 217 LB.
DEBUT: 3-28-19
TEAM: SAN DIEGO PADRES (2019–)
BORN: 1-2-99, SAN PEDRO DE MACORIS, SAN PEDRO DE MACORIS PROVINCE, DOMINICAN REPUBLIC

AVG	OBP	SLG	OPS+	HR	RBI
.292	.369	.596	160	81	195

Mike Trout

Baseball is a sport in which it can sometimes be hard to say one player is better than another; judging players often forces you to make apples-to-oranges comparisons. One player, for example, may be a better hitter for power, while another may be a better hitter for average. One may be a superior defender and base runner, while another is good at a number of things. Because of all the variables, it has not always been possible at a given time in baseball history to say that one player is, unequivocally, the greatest. It can, however, be confidently said that Mike Trout has been the greatest baseball player in the world since his major league debut and already stands as one of the greatest in baseball history.

Trout was a first-round draft pick of the Los Angeles Angels in 2009 and was almost immediately considered the top prospect in the game. He was virtually unchallenged as a minor leaguer in his first two pro seasons, and the Angels called him up to the majors for a couple of months in 2011. He'd be on the big league club for good less than a month after the 2012 season began. That year he hit 30 homers, led the league in runs scored, stolen bases, and OPS+ and, overall, put up one of the finest seasons for any player under the age of 25 in the history of the game. Trout was the unanimous choice for the Rookie of the Year Award that year and came in second in the MVP Award voting. Over the next seven seasons Trout would win MVP three times and finish second in the voting three times. Even in an injury-shortened 2017 campaign Trout came in fourth in the voting and led the American League in five offensive categories.

The most notable thing about Trout's game is that there is not just *one* notable thing. He hits for average and for power. He is an amazingly patient hitter who will draw walks. Despite being a potent middle-of-the-order hitter, he has stolen over 200 bases and rarely gets caught. For most of his career he has played center field, which is among the most challenging and most important defensive positions, and he has always been a superior defender. He is, simply put, one of the best all-around players in the history of the game.

A series of nagging injuries began to hamper Trout in 2020 and cut short his 2021 and 2022 campaigns as well. Despite that, he still hit 40 homers in 2022, and had he been healthy all year, he'd have been in the thick of the MVP conversation once again. Though he is still only in his early 30s, he has already ensured induction into the Hall of Fame one day. The only question now is how healthy he will remain for the rest of his career and how much higher on the list of all-time greats he will climb.

POSITION: OUTFIELD
BATS: RIGHT
THROWS: RIGHT
HT/WT: 6'2", 235 LB.
DEBUT: 7-8-11
TEAM: LOS ANGELES ANGELS
BORN: 8-7-91, VINELAND, NJ

AVG	OBP	SLG	OPS+	HR	RBI
303	.415	.587	176	350	896

Trea Turner

In a game where power is everything, Trea Turner has shown that there's still room for speed. He is one of the game's fastest players, in fact, having been clocked at over 22 mph on a full sprint on multiple occasions in his big league career—which approaches Olympic sprinter speed. That speed has allowed him to lead the National League in stolen bases twice in his career, and he is the only player in the top 10 of active stolen base leaders who has played fewer than 10 seasons.

But Turner is not just about fast legs. Statistically speaking, he has been one of the best all-around players in the majors over the past three or four years, with a career line of .302/.355/.487 (OPS+ 122). He has consistently hit for a high average while providing above-average power to go with that speed, averaging 24 home runs and 44 stolen bases for every 162 games played in his career. He is tied for the all-time record for most cycles—hitting a single, a double, a triple, and a home run in one game—in his career, with three. Though he split time between two teams in 2021 due to a midseason trade to the Dodgers, Turner finished 2021 leading the majors with a .328 batting average and 195 base hits—all of this while playing a respectable shortstop.

It is Turner's multifaceted performance that has made him so valuable to both the 2019 World Series champion Washington Nationals and to two years' worth of Dodgers teams, which have won more regular season games than any other club. It is also the sort of performance that will serve Turner very, very well when he becomes a free agent prior to the 2023 season.

POSITION: SHORTSTOP
BATS: RIGHT
THROWS: RIGHT
HT/WT: 6'2", 185 LB.
DEBUT: 8-21-15
TEAMS: WASHINGTON NATIONALS (2015–21), LOS ANGELES DODGERS (2021–)
BORN: 6-30-93, BOYNTON BEACH, FL

AVG	OBP	SLG	OPS+	HR	RBI
.302	.355	.487	122	124	434

Justin Verlander

Justin Verlander, like Max Scherzer, has simply defied Father Time. Though he will turn 40 before the 2023 season begins, Verlander remains one of the top pitchers in the game and stands as one of the greatest pitchers of his era or any other.

Verlander was selected by the Tigers as the second overall pick of the 2004 draft out of Old Dominion University, and he quickly established himself upon his big league debut in his first full season, winning the 2006 AL Rookie of the Year Award and helping lead the Tigers to an improbable American League pennant. Neither postseason hardware nor winning has been in short supply in his career, as he won the 2011 MVP Award, the 2011 and 2019 AL Cy Young Awards, has been elected to the All-Star team nine times, and has appeared in the World Series four times—twice with the Tigers and twice with the Houston Astros.

While Verlander has been considered one of the top hurlers in the game for nearly two decades, his tenure in Houston has been particularly remarkable, both because of what he has accomplished at an advanced age for a top athlete and because of the massive impact he made after being acquired by the Astros from Detroit in August of 2017. The Tigers, going nowhere competitively at the time, traded Verlander to Houston as a means of saving some money. Verlander, newly invigorated upon joining a winning team, began his Astros career by going 9–0 in his first nine games with the club, including five regular season and four postseason victories, accompanied by a 1.23 ERA and 67 strikeouts in that span. The trade ended up being one of the most impactful in-season pickups in baseball history, and Verlander's truly historic late season run was capped by an Astros World Series victory.

As time has gone on, Verlander has continued to rack up achievement after achievement. He's one of only two pitchers in MLB history—the other being the great Don Newcombe—to have won MVP, Cy Young, and Rookie of the Year, and he is the *only* pitcher to have won an MVP, Rookie of the Year, and *multiple* Cy Young Awards. He is one of only six pitchers in MLB history with three career no-hitters, tossing no-nos in 2007, 2011, and 2019.

Some great players end their careers wondering if they'll be elected to the Hall of Fame one day. With Verlander's career still amazingly appearing to have no end in sight, his ticket to Cooperstown and baseball immortality was punched a long, long time ago.

POSITION: STARTING PITCHER
BATS: RIGHT
THROWS: RIGHT
HT/WT: 6'5", 235 LB.
DEBUT: 7-4-05
TEAMS: DETROIT TIGERS (2005–17),
    HOUSTON ASTROS (2017–)
BORN: 2-20-83, MANAKIN-SABOT, VA

W	L	ERA	ERA+	IP	K	BB
244	133	3.24	132	3163	3198	880

Statistics Glossary

Each player in this book has a grid of some key statistics. One set is for hitters and another is for pitchers. Here is a brief explanation of what those statistics represent.

FOR HITTERS

Batting Average (BA): A player's hits divided by the total times at bat. High batting averages are considered to be .300 and above.

On-base percentage (OBP): How often a batter has been on base, calculated by adding together a batter's hits, walks, and the number of times he's been hit by pitches, then dividing that number by his at bats plus walks plus the times he's been hit by pitches plus his sacrifice flies. It's more advanced than batting average. Over .350 is excellent. Over .400 is absolutely outstanding.

Slugging percentage (SLG): A measure of effectiveness of a player's offensive efforts, measured by taking the total number of bases a player gets to divided by his at bats. SLG measures how powerful a hitter is, keeping in mind that home runs are worth more than triples, which are worth more than doubles, which are worth more than singles.

OPS+: A measure of a player's total offensive contribution, achieved by adding on-base percentage and slugging percentage together and then adjusting that number in a way that compares the player to other hitters in the league. An OPS+ of 100 is league average. So anything above 100 is above average, and anything below 100 is below average. A score of 150 is 50 percent better than the league average, a score of 85 is 15 percent below league average, and so on.

Home runs (HR): A four-base hit, usually accomplished by hitting the ball over the fence or into the stands. There are a lot of nicknames for home runs, including homer, dinger, tater, round tripper, bomb, and blast.

Runs batted in (RBI): An RBI is awarded to a batter whenever a runner on base or the batter themselves scores as a result of the batter's plate appearance, usually by a hit, a walk, or a sacrifice fly. 100 or more RBI in a season is outstanding.

FOR PITCHERS

Wins (W): A pitcher receives a win when he is the pitcher at the time his team takes the lead for good in a game. For many years winning 20 games in a season or 300 in a career was considered outstanding. Because of various changes in the game regarding how pitchers are used, these days 15 wins or more in a season or 200 wins in a career is considered a more reasonable standard of excellence.

Losses (L): The flip side of a win: when the player is the pitcher at the time the team falls behind for good. Even the best pitchers lose several games a year. Importantly, a pitcher can